# Facebook for Authors, Artists, and Entrepreneurs

## Social Networking for the Creative Mind

Lisa Shea

Content copyright © 2017 by

Lisa Shea / Minerva Webworks LLC

All rights reserved


No part of this book may be reproduced in any form or by any electronic or mechanical means including information storage and retrieval systems, without permission in writing from the author. The only exception is by a reviewer, who may quote short excerpts in a review.

~ v1 ~

All copyrights mentioned are owned by their respective owners.

# CONTENTS

Introduction ........................................................................... 1

Chapter 1 – The Basics ......................................................... 3

Chapter 2 – Creating the Account ......................................... 4

    Signing Up for Facebook ................................................. 5

    Facebook Profile Image ................................................... 7

    Banner Customization ................................................... 15

    Profile Customization ................................................... 16

    That's It! ........................................................................ 17

Chapter 3 – Personal Account vs Business Fan Pages ........... 18

    What Is A Personal Account? ....................................... 19

    What Is A Business Fan Page? ..................................... 20

    Using a Personal Page for Business Purposes .............. 22

Chapter 4 – Getting Images Ready to Post .......................... 26

    Take a High Quality Photo ........................................... 27

    Enhancing the Photo ..................................................... 30

    Storing the Photo .......................................................... 31

Chapter 5 – Business Page .................................................. 32

    Creating the Business Page .......................................... 33

Customizing your Business Page ........................................... 36

Chapter 6 – Making Posts ............................................................ 39

Making a Facebook Post ........................................................ 40

Image Details .......................................................................... 41

Posting a Link ......................................................................... 42

Posting Hand-Made Artwork Images .................................... 48

Liking a Post ........................................................................... 52

Why Likes Matter ................................................................... 56

Order of Posts on your Page .................................................. 57

Editing a Post .......................................................................... 58

Deleting a Post ........................................................................ 59

Chapter 7 – Tagging ..................................................................... 61

Tagging with a Personal Account .......................................... 62

Chapter 8 – Hashtags ................................................................... 65

What Is a Hashtag? ................................................................. 66

Hashtags and Artists ............................................................... 68

Finding Hashtags to Use ......................................................... 70

Holiday Hashtags .................................................................... 71

Chapter 9 – Sharing ..................................................................... 72

Chapter 10 - Your Timeline .................................................. 74

Chapter 11 - Advanced Posting Topics ................................. 75

    Auto-Posting from Other Systems ....................................... 76

    Multiple Posting of the Same Message ................................ 77

Chapter 12 - Building Followers ............................................ 78

    Followers Basics ................................................................. 79

    Building Traffic .................................................................... 81

    The Value of Followers ....................................................... 83

    Collaborate with Friends ..................................................... 85

    Followers who Bother You .................................................. 86

    Potential Contacts who Won't Accept ................................. 87

Chapter 13 – Messages ........................................................ 89

    Messages Basics ................................................................ 90

    Who You Can Message? .................................................... 91

Chapter 14 – Groups ............................................................. 92

    Creating a Group ................................................................ 93

Chapter 15 - Advanced Tips ................................................. 95

    Optimal Images for Likes .................................................... 96

    Motivational Quotes ............................................................ 98

Use the Word "Like" .......................................................... 99

Getting More Comments ................................................... 100

Play with Different Times ................................................. 101

Run Contests .................................................................... 102

Chapter 16 – Issues to Avoid ................................................. 103

Stealing Content .............................................................. 104

Repeated Hammering of a tag .......................................... 105

Banning ........................................................................... 106

Chapter 17 - Multiple Accounts ............................................ 107

Chapter 18 – Actually Reading Posts ................................... 108

Search Key Words ........................................................... 109

Chapter 19 –Facebook Ads ................................................... 110

Creating a Facebook Ad .................................................. 111

Defining your Ad Market ................................................ 115

Ad Placements ................................................................. 120

Ad Budget ....................................................................... 122

Ad Design ........................................................................ 124

The Review Process ........................................................ 127

Ads Manager ................................................................... 128

Changing an Ad .................................................................. 130

Chapter 20 - Lisa's Account .................................................. 133

Chapter 21 - Summary .......................................................... 134

Free Ebooks ........................................................................ 136

Dedication ........................................................................... 143

Glossary .............................................................................. 144

About the Author ................................................................. 145

"You can have everything in life you want if you will just help enough other people get what they want"

--Zig Ziglar

# INTRODUCTION

Did you know, when Facebook first appeared back in February 2004, that it was designed specifically as a way for Harvard college students to stay in touch? Back then it didn't even let in other people. It was a closed network.

Of course, over time, other students wanted in, and as they graduated they didn't want to leave the system.

Now Facebook is world wide, for all teens and adults, and it boasts a user base of nearly 2 billion active user accounts. Think about that. The entire world contains only 7.4 billion people. That is a staggering number of people all using one social network to interact.

The marketing ramifications of this are *huge*.

Let's get started!

Half of all proceeds of this book benefit local children's art programs.

Note: If you also have my Twitter book (or one of my other social networking books), you'll find that certain categories of this information overlaps. For example, the theory behind high quality eye-catching image design is fairly standard across the web. I aim to keep those types of sections similar across these books so that a person reading, for example, the Instagram book and then the Twitter book can see where those two relate. This can help a lot with cross-posting activities.

My aim is that, by reading this book, you'll be learning a foundation which you can then apply to many other social networking projects.

## CHAPTER 1 – THE BASICS

Facebook is everywhere. Grandparents use it to talk to their grandkids. Lovers use it to stay in touch from half-way around the world. It works on phones, tablets, laptops, and desktop computers. Movies have been made about it. Countless TV shows reference it.

It is a marketer's dream.

Facebook lets you target people in ways few could possibly dream of until now. By age. By location down to a village. By specific interests, TV shows, and movies. By pets. You name it.

Even if you don't "like" Facebook for personal use, you really need to use it for marketing reasons.

We'll work through all of this step by step.

Let's get started!

## CHAPTER 2 – CREATING THE ACCOUNT

The very first step in any project is to begin. To start with Facebook, it's time to create your account.

If you've already created an account, read through here to see if there were any steps you missed.

NOTE: You can only have ONE AND ONLY ONE personal account on Facebook. That's it. No matter how many pen names or companies or anything else you have, you can only have one personal account and it must have your REAL NAME on it. To do anything else is to risk it being deleted. The last thing you need, after building up a network of contacts and fans on Facebook is to lose them all in the blink of an eye.

Follow their rules on this. I've seen numerous cases where people have been devastated by the loss. Make an account with your real name. There are plenty of ways to set up groups and pages for your band, pen name, soap business, etc. once you have your main account set.

You don't even have to "use" your main account to post anything. You can keep it completely private. But you must have that main account in existence, with your real name, to serve as the administrator for the other accounts.

## SIGNING UP FOR FACEBOOK

To begin with, you need to go to the Facebook website at http://www.Facebook.com.

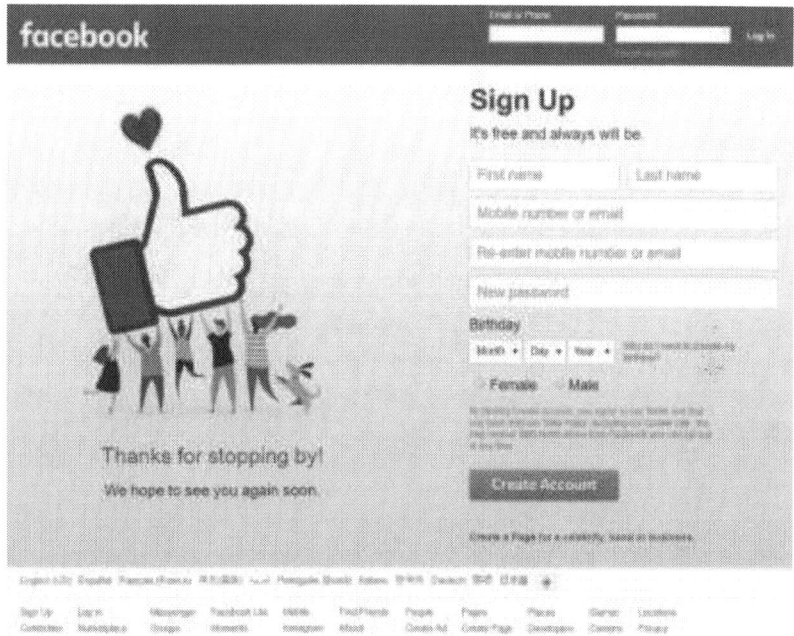

Facebook is awesome. You would think they'd have to be, with the massive user base they have. Right there they ask you for the key details.

USE YOUR REAL NAME. Again, you don't want to risk having everything get deleted for breaking their rules. You can use "Jimmy" if you go by Jimmy and not James, but you need to use the actual name you go by and not a fake one.

Fill in the details. I know there's a link to "create a page" but don't do it. They will make you have the administrator account anyway. It's much better to do this in order.

Once you click "Create Account", Facebook will send you a confirmation code. Click the link in the email to confirm your account.

Next up, you'll be taken to a page to help you find friends. You can either search by name or connect to your email account to find them that way. If you want to connect with friends then by all means start connecting. Otherwise feel free to ignore this part. There is plenty of time to connect with them later if you wish to.

On to the profile photo!

## FACEBOOK PROFILE IMAGE

The next step is for Facebook to get a profile image of you.

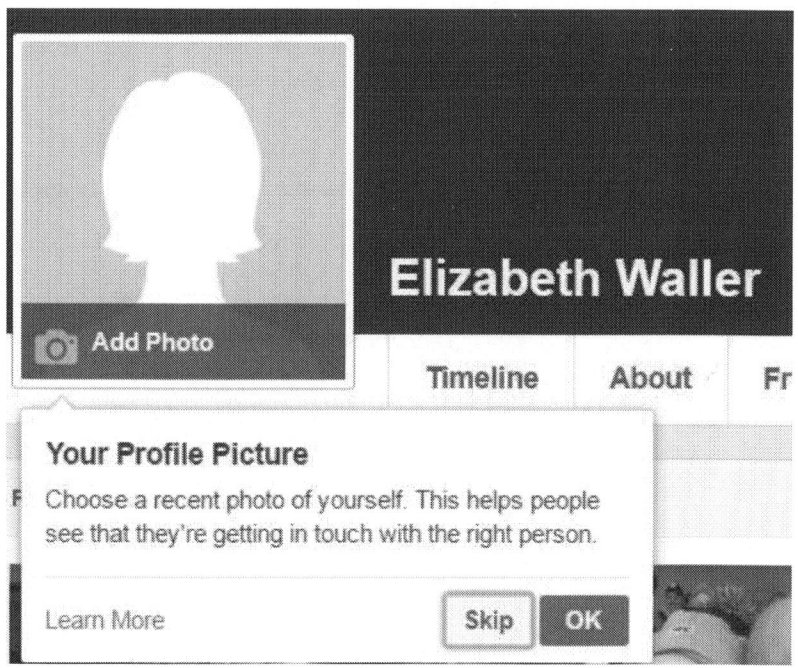

Facebook is one of the only social networks still using a square image. They don't like circles, apparently.

While this says to use a photo of yourself, quite a lot of people on Facebook put in images of cats, dogs, toys, you name it. Especially if you're just creating a profile in order to run a business page, feel free to skip this for now.

However, I do want to make a case for filling in the details for this personal account and simply USING it as a business account. So in that case, putting either a professional headshot or a company logo of some sort would work well.

Again, to reiterate, the NAME on the account must be real. But you can use this account as a way to talk to people about your business interests. I will get into that shortly, after we get this basic account set up.

Back to the photo itself.

If you've read my Twitter book you'll find this section here is nearly the same, for a clear reason – the image serves the exact same purpose on both platforms.

So, with that being said …

A main thing you are doing with Facebook is expanding the branding of you as a writer, artist, or however you wish to become known. Therefore it's critical that you choose an icon that continues your branding.

Make sure the photo you choose is square and clearly visible at the small size. Remember, many Facebook users are using this software on their phones. Your photo is going to be the size of a gnat on there. It has to be recognizable at that tiny size. If you want the image to show you as a person, don't show a full body image - show just a close-up on the face.

Make sure the photo is well taken. If the photo is fuzzy or out of focus it is going to give a poor impression to your readers. People really do care about those sorts of issues. People react very strongly to images.

Remember, your icon shows up next to EVERY POST YOU MAKE. That is a huge amount of promotion. It needs to do a good job.

I would NOT use a stock photo or generic image. Again, this is all about branding. Branding your name and words with a stock photo or image is anti-branding. :) It will do you no good in the long run. People are keyed to visual images and if you are building your reputation as a writer you can use every boost you can get! Definitely use your photo, and make it the best photo you can get. It is far better to use a photo and later upgrade to a "better photo" than to have a generic, meaningless image that will not provide any value to you.

Whatever you do, if you are going to be posting at all with this account, don't stay with the initial "head." The default image for a brand new Facebook account is a bland head image. This is a sign of a spammer and many people automatically ignore these accounts. Make sure you replace that default image as soon as possible.

This set of examples are for my WorcesterMA page, to show the steps I took there. The examples are for a circular image, for Twitter, but the thought progression is the same.

When I was setting up a page for a site about Worcester, I first went with an iconic landmark. It was an interesting idea - but at the tiny size this turned into a meaningless blur. That wasn't good.

Next, I tried the words with blue-on-yellow. But at the small size this turned into illegible fuzz.

I tried a thinner style of letter. This was better at the small size, but still hard to read.

So I changed the blue letters to black. Voila, suddenly it became much easier to read.

Still, it didn't seem to have much personality. My point for the Worcester MA site was to promote local events and fun. So I worked on making the letters in WORCESTER MA fit into a clock face. Voila! That's what I wanted and it worked on large and small sizes.

Note that for Twitter in the circle version the stars get trimmed out, but having it in a shape that works well for square and circle both means I can use this on various social networks and it is all right.

Once you settle on an image, it's best to stick with it. People will come to associate your image with you as an account. They'll look for that image and when posts come through their stream they'll recognize it. If you then randomly change your image every week, they'll lose that ability. They will not have as strong a connection with your posts.

So while it's good to experiment until you get a great image that works well at small sizes, once you find one, stick with it.

So, back to Facebook and setting this up.

You can leave the profile image blank if you really don't intend to use this personal account for any connections. You can always change it later.

## BANNER CUSTOMIZATION

Just as with pretty much every other social network, you also get a top banner image to customize. You can load it in now or skip over it.

This could be where you promote your books, your works of art, your products, or whatever else you're working on.

You can load up an image if you want – the size is 851 pixels wide by 315 pixels high. Again, this will only matter if you plan on posting as you as a person. Feel free to skip for now.

## PROFILE CUSTOMIZATION

The next thing Facebook does is ask you a bit about yourself. Because this started as a college-student-specific network, the first question is about college. That's a bit depressing for the people who didn't go to college and aren't happy about that. I wish they didn't start that way.

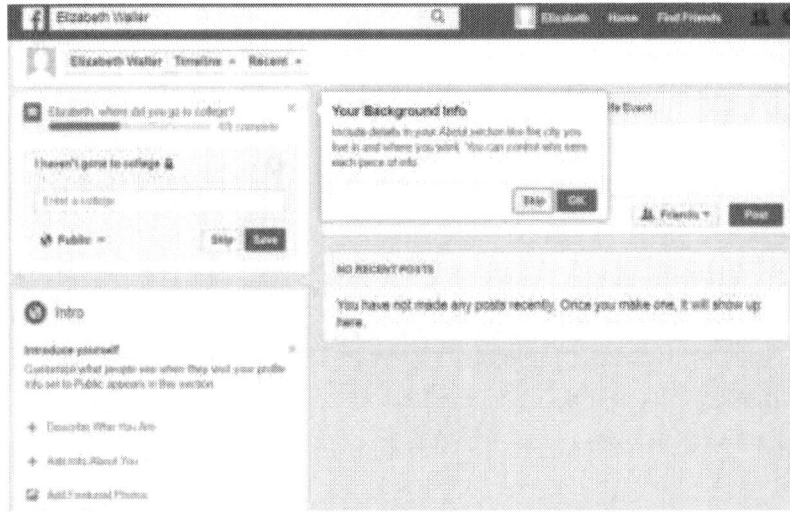

In any case, you can skip this all if you wish.

## THAT'S IT!

There you go! You have a spot for a profile image, a skeleton of a network, and a spot for a banner image.

Now it's time to start using your new Facebook account.

Let's get started!

## CHAPTER 3 – PERSONAL ACCOUNT VS BUSINESS FAN PAGES

Before you start posting, it's good to understand what a personal account is and a business fan page. This will make a difference in how and where you post.

## WHAT IS A PERSONAL ACCOUNT?

This thing you just set up is a personal account. It's how you log into Facebook. It identifies you as an administrator. You as an administrator can own one business fan page or lots and lots of business fan pages. Those fan pages look, to visitors, like a "business" – your personal account is entirely shielded from them. So this personal account lives in complete anonymity.

You can, of course, choose to make friends with this personal account. You can choose to customize it. But that's a choice. You can also choose NOT to friend anyone at all and simply use this as an administration account. That is quite fine.

The vast majority of people who are using Facebook are using one of these personal accounts to talk with friends and family with. They also use their personal account to interact with fan pages.

## WHAT IS A BUSINESS FAN PAGE?

A business fan page (I'll use both of these terms for this type of page) is a business / organization / etc. page. It is a page for an entity to connect with its fans. My RomanceClass website has a fan page. When people ask questions to RomanceClass they have no idea that "Lisa Shea" is behind it. They simply see the RomanceClass page with its logo and so on. They have no way of seeing or connecting with my Lisa Shea personal account.

That layer of privacy and protection is part of what fan pages are all about.

Fan pages can make posts, collect followers, interact with fans, and so on. You definitely want to have a fan page for your business for a few reasons.

First, it is in Facebook's explicit rules. If you set up a personal account with a fake name or with a business name in the "first name / last name" fields, once they find you, they'll shut you down. And you'll lose all those fans and posts you've built up.

Second, you can only have 5,000 friends for a personal account on Facebook. That might sound like a lot now, but hopefully your business projects will get you more fans than that soon enough. You wouldn't want to be turning away fans because they're trying to connect to a personal account.

Third, there is a difference in the way personal pages and fan pages connect with accounts. This gets a little tricky, so I'll try to explain this carefully.

Let's say two friends both have personal accounts, as normal. One is Lisa Shea and the other is Bob Smith. Lisa Shea will make a friend request to Bob Smith. Bob Smith accepts the friend request. Now Lisa and Bob can see everything the other person posts. They can see all the sleepy 2am posts. All the photos of people in pajamas. All that type of goofy stuff that happens.

But most people don't want to reveal all of that kind of stuff to a business they interact with. They don't want the business owners seeing photos of them in their pajamas.

So when a person "likes" a business page, the connection is far more restricted. Let's say Lisa Shea likes "Blue Bike Shop". If Blue Bike Shop makes posts, Lisa will see those in her timeline. But if Lisa makes posts, Blue Bike Shop does NOT see those posts. Blue Bike Shop does NOT see her photos. The person's privacy is maintained.

So it's important for businesses to set up fan pages because, honestly, most personal accounts will not *want* to "friend" a business. The people don't want a business seeing all their personal stuff. The people want to stay in touch, but in a way that protects their privacy.

Feel free to ask me if this is still a bit confusing.

## USING A PERSONAL PAGE FOR BUSINESS PURPOSES

Let me reiterate again that you don't have to do this. You can keep your personal page completely empty and solely maintain the business pages.

You can also keep your personal page wholly personal and only use it to talk about personal things with family and friends.

But there's a third route – one I take because of the enormous marketing opportuity.

I use my personal page as another way of marketing. Yes, sometimes I put personal posts in there – but only ones I'm comfortable going to my entire fan base. Most of what I post about are within my sphere of business activities – my yoga, my meditation, the books I'm writing, and so on.

Let's take a look at this and see how it works.

Here is how my profile page is set up. You can see it online here:

https://www.facebook.com/lisashea.origami

So the picture is of me. It's my actual name, of course, as required. And the top image banner promotes my books. The intro promotes my books and other projects.

I have nearly 5,000 friends. That's at the limit. But while some of those are friends and family, the vast majority are other authors. They hear about my latest book releases and help to promote them. We talk about book marketing ideas. I use this account as a public writing group network.

I set all of my posts to be fully public. Again, this is with the mindset that this is a public blog of my writing and not a personal account. I would not post anything on here that I wanted to hide from the world.

This gets me enormous reach for my posts and great interaction with other people who can help me grow (and who I can help grow).

Now, again, this is wholly your choice about how to use Facebook. You can keep this personal area as private for you and your friends and family. You can choose not to post anything at all in the personal area. For marketing reasons, though, I advocate the third path. I advocate using it as a blog and posting things you wish to get marketed.

Now, here is the Lisa Shea Author business page I have set up on Facebook. You can see this here:

https://www.facebook.com/LisaSheaAuthor

See how similar it is? But this one is a business page. People can "like" it without making that personal connection. I'm allowed far more than 5,000 followers here. They can sign up for my newsletter. See links to my books. Easily share the news about book releases.

From my point of view, I can reach a larger group of people. Host events. There are all sorts of things a business page can do that a personal page can't do.

So whether or not you choose to use that personal page area for anything, we're going to focus on making the business page, because that will be important for everyone reading this book.

But first we're going to talk a bit about images, as they are critical to success on Facebook.

## CHAPTER 4 – GETTING IMAGES READY TO POST

Images are immensely popular on the web. Every post on Facebook needs to have an image in order to catch the eye. When people are scrolling – scrolling – scrolling on their timeline, it's the image that gets them to stop.

While you can certainly post raw photos right out of your camera or phone, it's worthwhile to do a bit of editing to the image. That way you put your best foot forward in the marketing of your brand.

## TAKE A HIGH QUALITY PHOTO

Facebook is a very visual system. And while lots of people use Facebook on their small smartphones, many people do use Facebook on large-screen computers. They will be able to appreciate the fine detail on the higher quality image. They will be far more likely to like and remember that image. It's well worth it for you to give them that high quality image if at all possible.

That means, then, having a camera that can take photos of that pixels level or larger.

Yes, many smartphones have that ability, but in many cases you'll want to be able to adjust the aperture to create a soft, fuzzy background. That lets the viewer focus on the main aspect of the image.

Perhaps you'll want to be able to adjust the shutter speed to capture motion just right.

These are often tasks handled with great precision by larger-sized cameras with more specialized controls and larger lenses. Especially if you are aiming to sell a product or entice someone with a book cover, you want to ensure that image is as perfect as possible.

A good camera doesn't have to be incredibly expensive. If you do your research you can find one that has the controls you need within your budget, especially if you look on eBay or other similar sites.

Also, try talking with local camera clubs. Maybe you can work with someone there and have them take some photos for you in exchange for something.

If the item you're taking a photo of *is* a piece of art, like a watercolor painting or a sculpture, there are entire books and classes on how to do that well. Do some web research to start. It's critical you use proper lighting and setup to get everything to represent well on the JPG / RAW file version.

However you do it, getting those high quality photos is a key first step. Facebook is quite attentive to professional image, since it is primarily about jobs and marketing. If you have a low quality, poorly lit, fuzzy image, it will harm you rather than help you.

## ENHANCING THE PHOTO

Sure, master photographers can take the one perfect photo, have it cropped perfectly, and go with that without touching. However, for the rest of us we need to do some tweaking.

I use Photoshop myself. I have friends who use Lightroom and other programs. Find a program that works well for you and learn all of its abilities. You might be amazed at how subtle changes in contrast and light balance can really make a photo or image pop.

It's worth it to at least take a run at it in your editing program of choice to see if you can improve the image. Remember, once you post it, this will represent you and your brand. If you're an author it might not be the end of the world if your book cover is slightly dark – but if you're an artist, that's your end product there on the screen.

## STORING THE PHOTO

Always, always, always store a copy of your photo on your local system or your cloud account. Don't just have it on your phone! Phones get lost, dropped, stolen, you name it. Always keep backups.

It's a good idea to develop a storage organization system that works for you. Many people do it by date and then subject within the dates.

Whatever you do, stick with it. Don't just toss photos into random folders. You never know when you'll need one of those photos.

Also, back up regularly. I have one friend who keeps backup drives in a local safe deposit box. Photos are irreplaceable. You always want access to those original, full size images.

When you're ready to save the Facebook version, give it a name that indicates that. So perhaps Marigold-FB.jpg. That would be the final version. Never destroy that original file – you might want to use it again some other time.

Now that the image is ready, you're able to post!

But first, let's make that business page.

## CHAPTER 5 – BUSINESS PAGE

A business page, also called a fan page, is the way an organization or company or author can interact with fans in a way which protects the fans' privacy.

A given personal account can have as many fan pages as they wish. I would not make one for every book of an author, but I would make one for each of an author's pen names. That way the different accounts can be kept separate. I have I think 27 different Facebook fan pages. One for Lisa Shea Author, one for RomanceClass, one for Wine Intro, and so on.

Here's how to get started.

## CREATING THE BUSINESS PAGE

Start by going to any existing business page. For example, go to my author page:

https://www.facebook.com/LisaSheaAuthor

In the left-hand menu, near the bottom, will be a green button which says "Create a Page". Click that button.

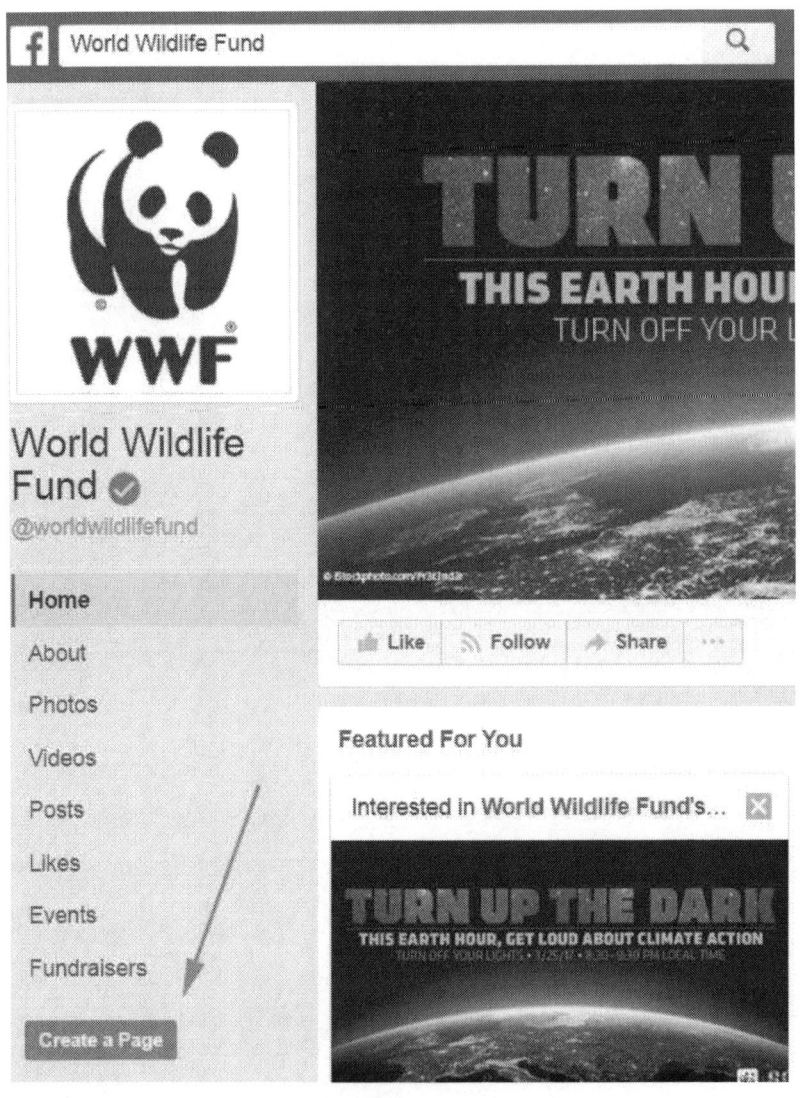

You'll be asked what kind of a page it is. Don't stress TOO much about this. A key difference for example is that a "local page" will be asked about the hours it's open while an artist page won't. So go with whatever seems to be best but don't obsess.

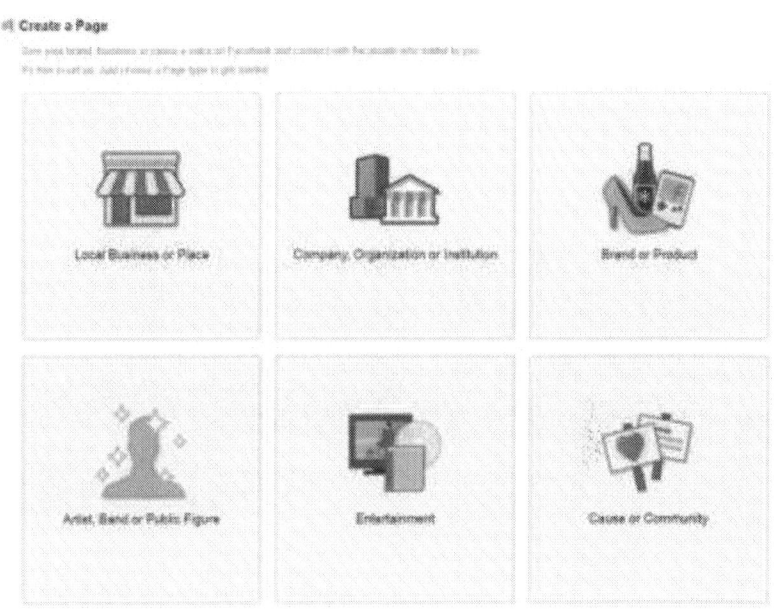

When you click on something you'll be asked for a name. Type in the name, of course.

Your page is now ready for customization!

## CUSTOMIZING YOUR BUSINESS PAGE

Your business page, just like your personal page, has a place for a profile image and a banner image. The descriptions of those from the personal page are pretty much the same here. Go with clear, meaningful images.

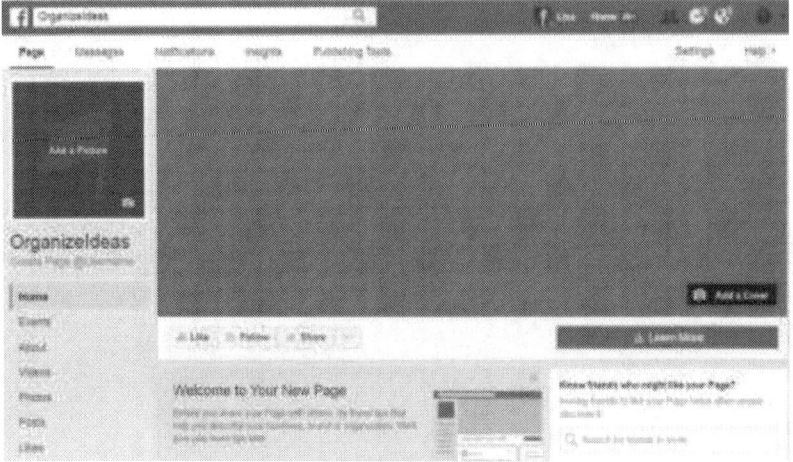

Once you put in a profile square and a top banner, you want to give your page a short, easy-to-use URL. You do that by clicking the link on the left beneath your profile photo.

The system will tell you if the name you want for your URL is already taken. Try to choose something easy to type and remember.

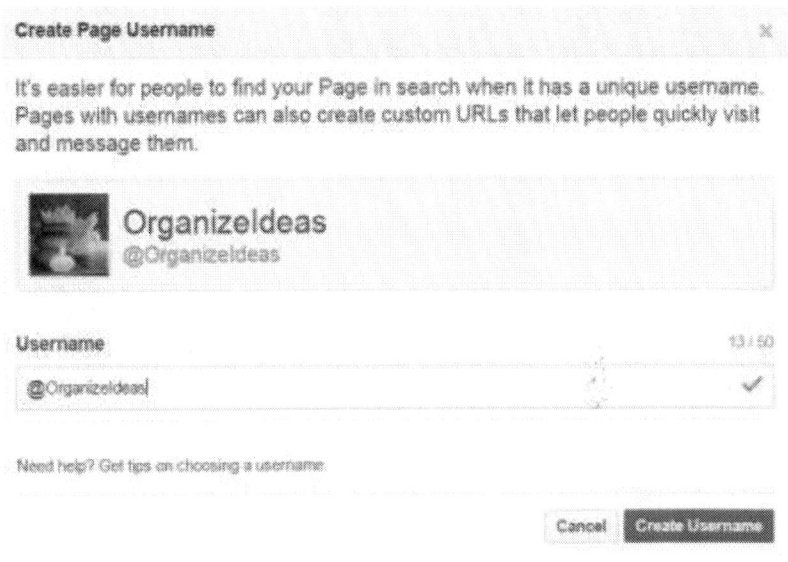

You can also add a short description for your site, as prompted.

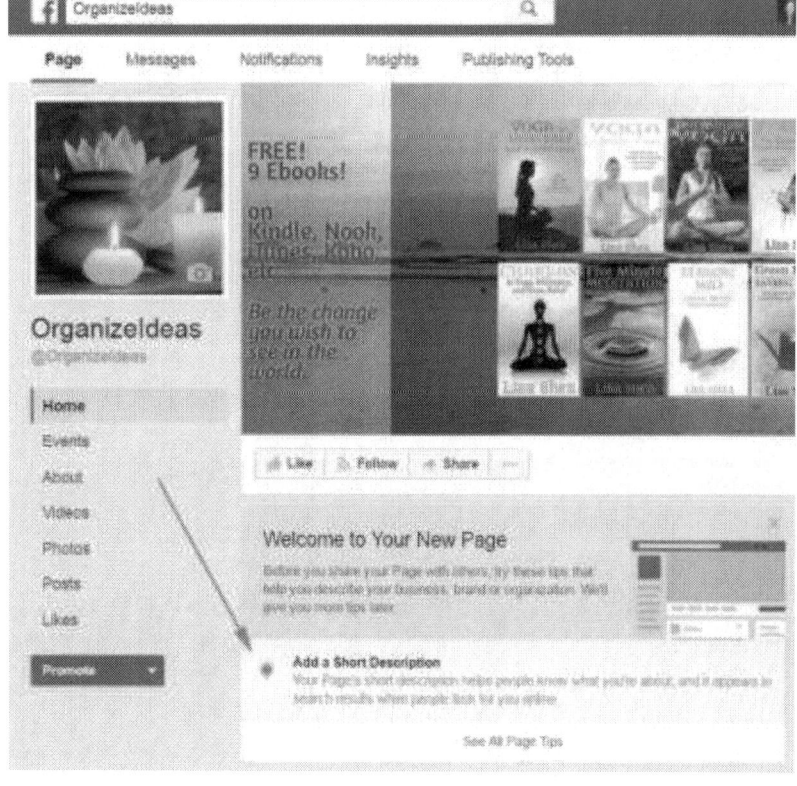

You're now ready to start posting!

## CHAPTER 6 – MAKING POSTS

Facebook allows members to make posts quickly and easily. There's a image-icon button to add an image to a post. The URL automatically gets linked to, just like in pretty much any other social network.

Let's explore the mechanics of making that post!

## MAKING A FACEBOOK POST

The mechanics of making a post on Facebook are very straightforward. Once you are logged into Facebook, and on your personal profile page or on any of your business fan pages, the very top center space is for you to type in your post. You simply type in your words and hit the POST button.

Voila, out it goes.

You do have the ability to delete it if you wish.

Let's talk about the process of creating a post.

**Your Post is Seen on your Page**
Anyone who goes to your page (either your personal or your business page, whichever you posted to) to learn more about you will see your post. Your posts are sorted in time order with the most recent post on the top. So if you make five posts on Saturday, all five posts will be on your page, with the most recent one on top.

**Your Post is Seen by your Followers**
Your followers have the option of seeing every single post made by every person they follow on their timeline. This is what I call the "firehose" - the massive flood of posts of every single person being followed.

Most of the time this isn't practical because there are just too many posts, once you move past following a few hundred people. But the post is there. It's in that stream.

Let's see how this all works.

## IMAGE DETAILS

If you post a link to an external URL, Facebook, like LinkedIn and Twitter, will auto-find an image on that page to use with the link. Sometimes that works well, if you're linking to a news site and the news article has a good image to go with it. Sometimes it works less well, like when you link to your brand new book on Amazon and Amazon hasn't gotten your cover to show up properly yet.

In general, always have a back-up image option. You want your post to have an image with it. Many times it's far better for you to customize the image to be exactly what you want, vs relying on the destination site to provide one for you.

### A Note about Images

Just like on LinkedIn and Twitter, it's common for people to use stock images that they've bought the rights to. If you post a motivational quote you can use a stock image of butterflies to go with it, as long as you own the rights to that image. Always make sure you purchase or secure rights for any image that you use.

If you are showing images of your products, of course, those should be pictures of your actual products and not stock images of someone else's products ☺.

## POSTING A LINK

So let's do an example of a link post, since that is a common use that you'll be using Facebook for. Let's say I'm an author and I want to post a link to my meditation book. I would go to my profile page or my business page, wherever I was going to make my post. In this example I'm on my business page, but the mechanics are exactly the same for the personal page .

Right there at the top of the page is a space for me to type in a new post.

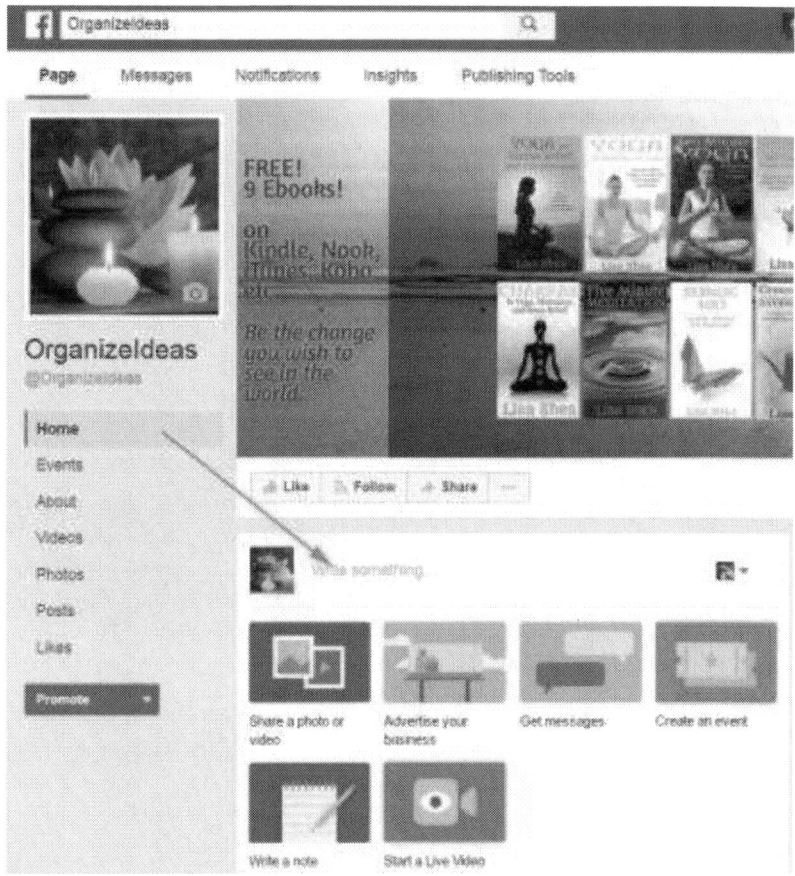

I don't just want to trust that when I put in a URL link to Amazon, my blog, or elsewhere, that it will give a full-format image that makes sense. So I want to use the camera icon to load up my own custom image, and then have text and a URL to go with it. Note the image is truncated in this screenshot.

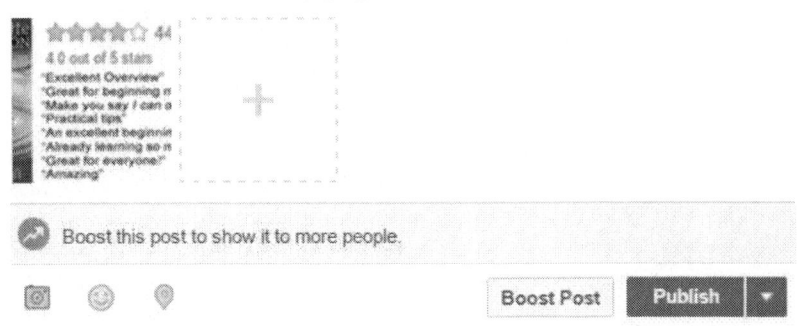

This is what it ends up looking like:

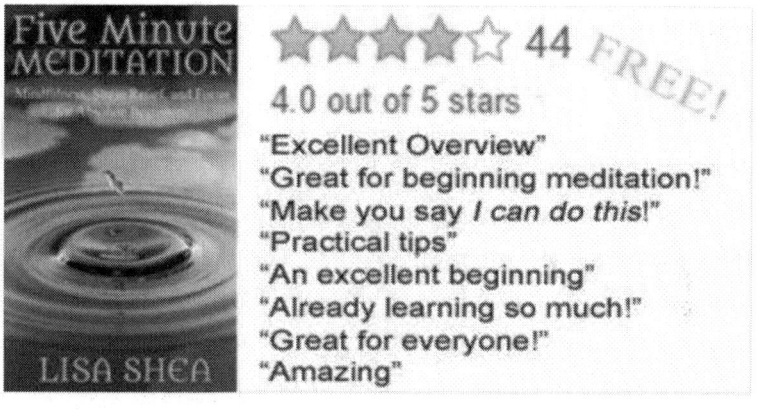

That whole section down beneath the top text is a big image – including the blurbs and the stars and everything. That's an image I made to do a good job of "selling" the book.

In comparison, if I just put in the top text without adding my own image, Facebook would auto-use an image it saw at the destination. Half the time it seems to get the wrong image, which is of course bad. And even if it gets the right image it can look like this:

**OrganizeIdeas**
Just now

FREE! Have you ever wanted to learn how to meditate? Have you heard how it improves focus and releases stress? This step by step book guides you every step of the way, and it's free! http://www.amazon.com/Five-Minute-Meditation-M.../.../B00VP90YEC Share the news!

★★★★★ (43 Reviews)

**Five Minute Meditation: Mindfulness, Stress Relief, and Focus for Absolute Beginners**

We've seen all the studies. Meditation helps with focus. With relieving stress. With warding off Alzheimer's, reducing colds, and improving nearly every aspect of life. But...

AMAZON.COM

Not awful – but not nearly as good as the hand-crafted one I made in terms of making the case for the book.

Don't worry about the "strange" truncated URL Facebook uses. It's just the way they shorten long URLs so they don't take over a post.

When you're making these posts you'll often have Facebook pushing you to "boost" the post. That means they want you to pay money ☺. Ignore those. If you ever do want to do marketing for your page, you do that through their ad system. Don't pay to boost posts. It's not economical compared with their actual ad system options.

So there is a basic post!

## POSTING HAND-MADE ARTWORK IMAGES

It's easy enough to post promotions of your images if you're a digital photographer. The file is already in digital form. You just get that file onto your camera, hit the post button, and you're all set.

As we mentioned in the previous chapter, what about when the item in question is analog? What if it's a watercolor painting, a cyanotype, a pencil drawing, or something else in the "tangible world"?

First, make sure the image is as perfect as humanly possible. If the lighting is poor, or the focus is fuzzy, people will move on. Remember, they have 80 billion other options out there. Yours has to hit them as *just right* for them to take action.

Yes, it's tricky to photograph art well. Take the time to practice and build up those skills. Learn how light and shadow can impact an image. Take the photo straight on to the object. Use PhotoShop or other tools to clean up the resulting image.

So this next one is a cyanotype I made. A cyanotype is made by painting light-reactive chemicals on a surface like paper, cloth, wood, or so on. You then lay objects down on that paper. The sun turns the areas it touches blue and the rest remain the natural color. So you're creating images from shadows of the sun.

So, to promote this, I posted a photo of my cyanotype and added text and a URL to my post. That is, I did NOT let

Facebook auto-add an image to go with the link. I made sure I loaded a photo that best represented that piece.

So, as you can see, Facebook shows that photo full-image. It didn't crop or mangle it.

As we've discussed, keep in mind that people searching Facebook can only search the words *associated with* an image.

That is, if they searched for the key word "cyanotype" and this photo had no description, this photo wouldn't come up as a result because "cyanotype" would be nowhere to be found in the text along with it. This might seem like common sense – but it's important to keep in mind!

If your photo is of a flower *use the word flower in your description*. Make sure your image can be found by people searching using the correct key words. If the photo shows a marigold, use the word *marigold* as a tag. And add it to a marigold group, if possible.

Also, if you are an artist aiming to make sales, make sure you always link in your description to or describe a sales destination for your photo or painting image. It can be FineArtAmerica, your own website, or any other place you want.

Yes, there will be thousands of people who love it but aren't interested in buying it for whatever reason. Maybe their walls are full. Maybe they're downsizing. That's all right. This is a volume game. You want to reach as many people as possible with your image so that the one person who *is* in a position to buy and who loves your style gets to see the image. And you want to make sure it's as easy as possible for that person to acquire their print before they get distracted by something else and don't finish the transaction.

Finally, keep a folder with the images and the descriptions you've used. It will help you keep track of which images you've already sent out and what types of descriptions seemed to work well.

## LIKING A POST

Let's say you see a post on Facebook that you appreciate. How do you show your support? You do that with a "like" which is fairly universal language across all social networking systems.

You like a post by clicking the "Like" thumbs-up icon beneath the post. That's it! Quick, simple, done. That indicates that you've liked the post. The author of that post can see your like.

Often they might say thank you or stop by your page to see what you're about.

Note that by default you will like as YOU the human being, from your personal page. If you want to like something as one of your business pages, you have to:

**World Wildlife Fund**
14 hrs

Mark your calendars and spread the word: Earth Hour will be taking place on March 25th at 8:30pm your local time! Landmarks like the Empire State Building are participating this year. Will you join them?

Click the drop-down option at the bottom right of the thing you're looking at. There you'll have the option to act as yourself or one of your various business pages. Just click on your business page name and then you can like, share, and comment as that business page.

Unfortunately, strangely, Facebook doesn't make it easy for you to see your liked posts in a neat list. In order to see what you have liked, you need to go to your profile link in the top right and look at your "Activity Log."

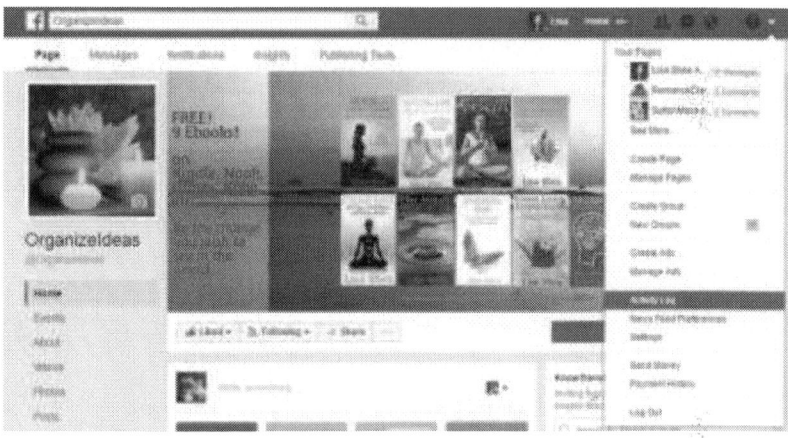

It shows you ALL activity though – the likes you've clicked ono, the posts you've made, etc. etc. So you have to manually weed through those in order to see the items you've liked.

## WHY LIKES MATTER

Likes are great for publicity reasons. Every like of your post raises its count of value.

When a given user looks at their "timeline" they see a massive stream of every post made by every person they follow. It can be a quick-flowing stream just jam-packed full of stuff. The same thing happens if a user looks for a search term or hashtag. They could be seeing tens of thousands of posts with more flowing in every second.

But Facebook gives different weights to different posts. If you look at the top of a search result, you'll see the most popular ones at the very top. These are the ones that have the most likes.

So it's well worth it to work to earn those likes. They directly impact how much your posts are seen.

## ORDER OF POSTS ON YOUR PAGE

Posts always show up in date order. The last item you post shows up on top.

## EDITING A POST

You made a post and when taking a second look at it you realize there's a typo in it.

How do you edit that post?

Go to your profile page and scroll to find the post you wish to edit. When you click your mouse in the top-right corner, in the "down arrow" a menu list of options will appear. One of those is edit.

Voila, edit away!

## DELETING A POST

You've made a post and realize in hindsight, really wasn't the best type of image to show publicly. You want to delete it.

How do you do that?

In the same Edit screen, simply click on the "delete from page" link.

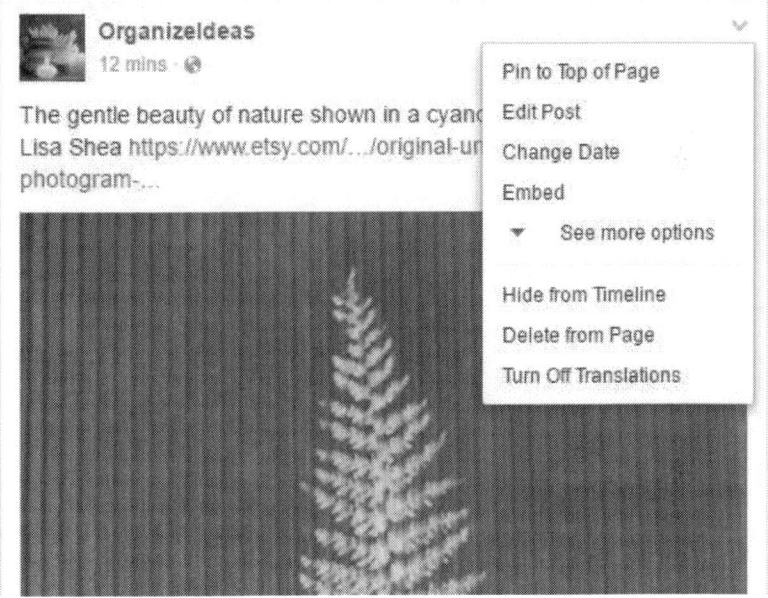

This gives you the delete option. Keep in mind that you'll lose all your likes and comments on it. But sometimes a post just needs to be deleted.

Note that you can also hide it from the timeline if you just don't want people to easily find it any more.

## CHAPTER 7 – TAGGING

Tagging on Facebook is different than hashtags and it's different from geotagging. It's about making a connection with another account.

Here's how tagging works on Facebook and how to use it.

## TAGGING WITH A PERSONAL ACCOUNT

Let's say you're making a post in your personal account and you want to give thanks to Joe Smith for the help he gave you on a project. You would type in his name as part of your text. Facebook will realize that Joe Smith is a friend of yours and highlight it to link to him.

He'll get an alert that he was tagged in the post, so he knows about it. Depending on his timeline settings, the post might even show up on his page.

People use this type of tagging for all sorts of reasons. They do it to give thanks or a shout-out to someone who helped them. If they see something interesting on Facebook, often they'll type that person's name into a comment – this then alerts the person to come take a look at the post.

Here's an example. I ran an ad for one of my books. This ad shows up in readers' timelines based on their interests. I'll get into how ads work later. But the thing to note is that people share and comment on the ad.

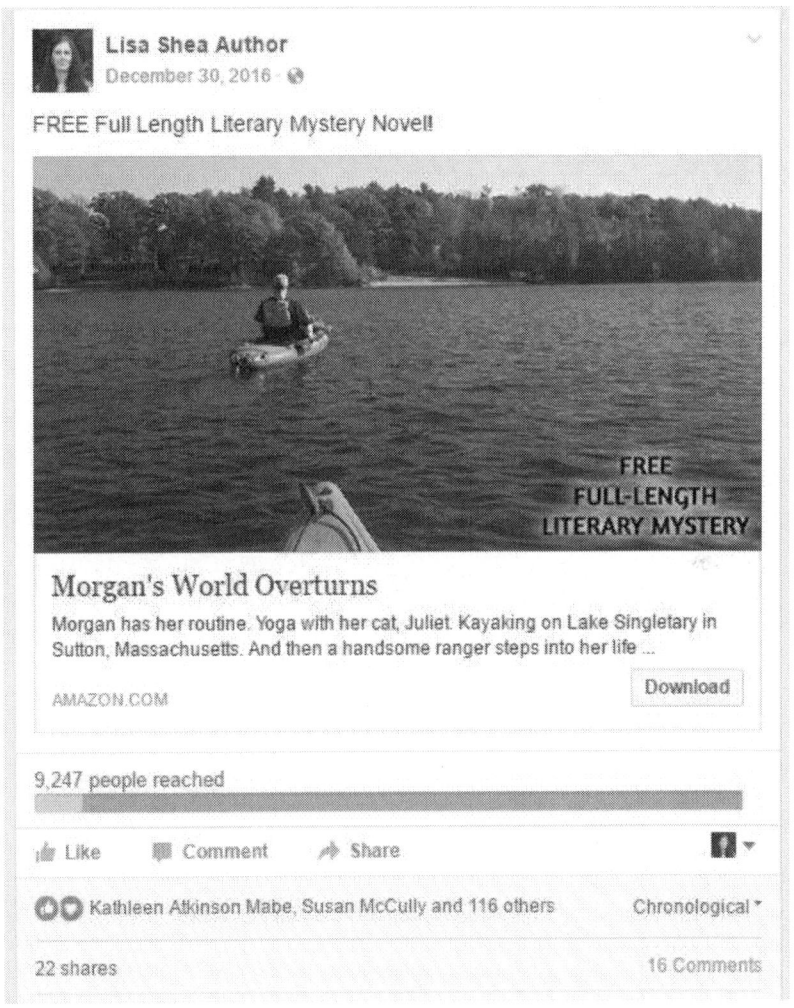

So in 22 cases people shared this ad onto their own page so their friends and family saw the ad. There are 16 comments on it. In many of those cases, the comment is one person, let's say Jane Smith, simply typing the name of a friend, Bobby Brown. When Jane makes that comment, Bobby gets an alert with a link to the post. So it's a way to quickly let a friend know about something interesting.

You can only tag someone you're actually connected to as a friend. You can't tag random people. This is set up this way to prevent spammers from harassing you all day long.

## CHAPTER 8 – HASHTAGS

In my Twitter book I cover hashtags quite early, as they are so integral to the Twitter experience. Here on Facebook, hashtags aren't nearly as important since the primary use of Facebook is to communicate with your network.

Still, hashtags are active in Facebook and it's good to know how they work.

## WHAT IS A HASHTAG?

Hashtags are most often equated with Twitter. But they have become used by other social networks such as Facebook as well. What are these hashtags all about, and why do people use them?

On Twitter, since Twitter has a short character limit for posts, hashtags were a way to quickly indicate what a post was about. I could make a post for a low carb recipe, add the hashtag #LowCarb at the end, and the post would easily be found by people who were searching for low carb ideas.

That same functionality is now used in other places which don't have the short text limitation.

Let's take a look at a post I made in Facebook:

**OrganizeIdeas**
Just now

FREE #yoga step by step instructions. This is my daily morning routine - I enjoy it immensely. http://www.amazon.com/Yoga-Stress-Relief-Forgiveness-Lis.../.../

32

**4.5 out of 5 stars**

"Excellent and easy to follow."
"A great book for an intro to yoga."
"Good easy poses. Will use often."
"Very good for beginners."
"Really good, enjoyed reading this."
"I really loved it. Great information!"
"A perfect introduction to the basics."

If someone then clicks on "#yoga" they see all posts made with that hashtag. And the more hashtags you have in your own posts, the more likely you are to be found in those cases.

I would stick with at most one or two hashtags on Facebook. For the longest time Facebook did not use hashtags at all. They're easing it in, but many people on Facebook still look at hashtags as a strange intruder to their world. So be gentle in your use of them.

## HASHTAGS AND ARTISTS

Hashtags are important for all posts. But for visual artists, they're especially important because people can't search on an image. They can't search on "orange" and find your image just because it happens to be an orange sunset or, heck, of a juicy orange slice. Search only works on words. If you are showcasing an image, you need to use hashtags in order for people to find it.

First comes the obvious. If you're showing an image of a sunset use the #sunset hashtag. If you're showing a zebra use #zebra. That way people who are looking for those hashtags can find your lovely photo or painting. If you have a bunch of #puffin photos be sure to tag them with #puffin. You might be surprised how many other #puffin lovers there are out there in the world.

But think beyond that. Maybe someone adores the color blue and they're looking for a #blue #painting. If your image is a multi-layered blue abstract painting you want to make sure you use those tags. What if someone loves #surreal art and that's what you like to paint? Make sure you use that hashtag in your description.

Be sure to use hashtags that people will search on, though. It doesn't do any good to tag your image with #PinkAndRedAcrylicPaintingOfDog if nobody is ever going to search on that tag. It would be a waste of precious characters.

Do some searches yourself, first, for words you think might relate to your image. See which ones get good results. Then incorporate those words into your own posts.

## FINDING HASHTAGS TO USE

You can of course try randomly searching on a hashtag like #cyanotype or #sweetromance or #sheabutter to see what comes up. That can be a good way to see if a hashtag is in common use or rarely used.

In general you want to aim for the commonly used ones. That being said, every once in a while it's fun to use one that is rarely used. It means your post will be seen by everyone who *does* look for it.

A great way to find hashtags is to look at other people in your genre. If you write cozy mysteries, track down a few cozy mystery authors. See what hashtags they use with their posts.

## HOLIDAY HASHTAGS

Holidays are prime reasons to post. You can plan for them, which helps out a lot. As the holiday approaches watch to see which hashtag people are using to tweet about it. That way your post gets seen by millions, vs using a hashtag that nobody is paying attention to.

For example, here's a post I made to tie in to #StPatricksDay

FREE on KindleUnlimited - Irish Romantic traditions perfect for #StPatricksDay! http://www.amazon.com/gp/product/B00UR53VOA

**Love, Irish Style**

"Lisa Shea reveals the true romantic Irish soul. Irish folklore is full of stories of the mating game, and there are traditions to guide us on every step of the process."
— M. E. Sweeney

## CHAPTER 9 – SHARING

Just like LinkedIn and Twitter, Facebook is built heavily around the concept of sharing. It actively encourages you to watch the Facebook timeline for posts you like and to share them to your own page. It's not that you're claiming you took those images or first saw that content. The posts ALWAYS link back to their source origin. It is that you are sharing the news about those great images.

So let's say I find a post I like. I first make sure I'm using Facebook as my page, if it's my desire to share the post to my page. That's done to the lower right of the post. Then I click on the "share" icon. It's at the bottom center of every post on Facebook. I'm then given the option to add some personal text to my share.

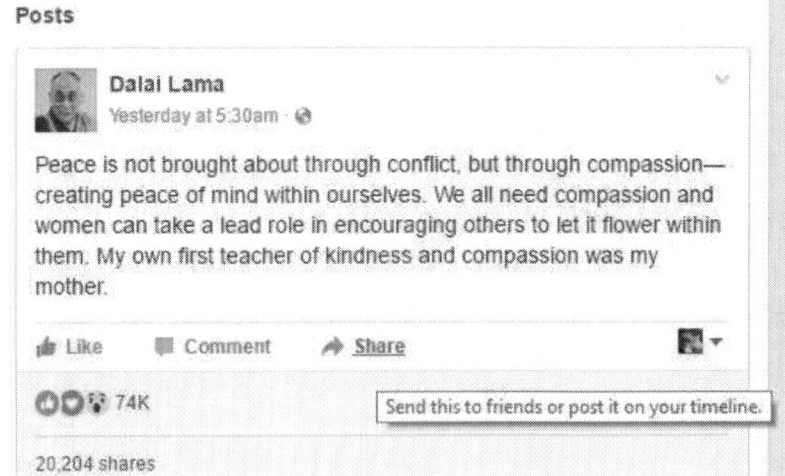

Voila, now this post is shared to my own network.

**Posts**

**OrganizeIdeas** shared Dalai Lama's post.
Just now

Words of wisdom.

Dalai Lama
Yesterday at 5:30am

Peace is not brought about through conflict, but through compassion—creating peace of mind within ourselves. We all need compassion and women can take a lead role in encouraging others to let it flower within them. My own first teacher of kindness and compassion was my mother.

## CHAPTER 10 - YOUR TIMELINE

I've talked several times about the ability to use Facebook without doing anything at all with your personal account area. If you do that, though, your Timeline will be empty. You won't have any news from friends, family, or pages to be alerted about.

What I might suggest, even if you don't want to make posts, is to follow pages that you are interested in. If you're an artist, maybe follow pages of artists who are doing a good job of marketing. That way you can occasionally check your timeline to get ideas about what to post.

You don't have to make any posts yourself, but it will put that timeline to good use.

The timeline only shows pages, groups, and personal accounts that your own personal account is following. It doesn't have anything to do with your business accounts.

## CHAPTER 11 - ADVANCED POSTING TOPICS

Most posting is fairly straightforward. You go to your Facebook account. If you're not already logged in, you log into your account. Either on your personal account page or on your business page, you click the post icon, find your image, and type something in. It gets posted. You're done.

Here are some advanced topics in the world of Facebook posting.

## AUTO-POSTING FROM OTHER SYSTEMS

It can be quite tempting. You're posting anyway on LinkedIn, Twitter, or another system. Why not just have that other system update Facebook for you?

Just say no.

Facebook has its own quirks. The way hashtags work, for example

Also, when you post on Facebook, people can respond *immediately*. In seconds. And when they comment you want to respond quickly. Otherwise they move on to something else and forget all about you.

Be present when you're on Facebook. Be there, make your post, and watch the results.

You might be surprised how many responses you get.

## MULTIPLE POSTING OF THE SAME MESSAGE

On other systems like Twitter it's common practice to keep reposting the same thing. The theory is that someone might not have seen the post the first time around. You're giving them another opportunity.

On Facebook it's more like you're having a conversation with friends. And having the same link over and over again in a collection is quite redundant.

Avoid duplicate posting. Find new things to post instead.

## CHAPTER 12 - BUILDING FOLLOWERS

Posting links and images can be fun, but it's also nice to have a stable of loyal followers to support you and encourage you.

Here is how to increase your number of followers.

## FOLLOWERS BASICS

It's important to build up your list of followers on Facebook. These tend to be the key people who support and like you. How do you build up a large list of high quality followers?

To start with, as long as this isn't a pen name or other secret type of account, I do recommend connecting your Facebook account to Twitter, LinkedIn, and other networks in terms of sharing names. This can bring you in hundreds to thousands of fans instantly. Just about everybody and their brother are on Facebook.

Next up, if you're using your personal account for posts, watch for the people who make connection requests. You'll see those names by clicking on the "Friend Request" two-head icon in the top menu bar.

Note that, like LinkedIn, Facebook has the concept of a "connection" and a simple "follower" for a personal page. Someone can follow you to see what's in your public timeline. They can also ask for a connection (a "friendship") which is a mutual relationship.

Facebook tells you your follower count on your profile page, under "profile photo" – click to see who they are.

To see your actual friends, click on "Friends" beneath your main banner page.

So far so good. Now take a look at the latest post you made. Let's say it's of a cyanotype. Go search on the word *cyanotype* and start liking and following the authors of the results you like. You can do that as your page, if you want to keep your profile private. When they see your like show up, they often will come by your page to see what you do. When they see you also make cyanotypes, they're likely to follow you back.

## BUILDING TRAFFIC

Building traffic for your Facebook feed is almost exactly the same as building traffic for any other social networking system. A small investment of time can result in a HUGE impact on traffic flowing to your site and income flowing to your pocketbook.

## UDPATE OFTEN
It's not really necessary to update daily, if you don't generate that type of output, because people tend to watch their main timeline and often there are too many posts for them to keep up with anyway.

With that being said, don't go weeks and weeks without posting. People will forget about you. If you can post daily, that's great! Especially if you can work your way slowly through an archive of images.

If you're just creating a painting, post updates showing what you're doing. People love that sort of thing.

If you're an author, post inspiring quotes and bits of the story.

For store owners, post about your latest products.

If you find that type of creative challenge rough, talk to friends and family for ideas. Keep a notebook on you to jot down ideas. Read your email to see what people are asking about. The ideas are out there.

**MENTION IN YOUR NEWSLETTER**
Every time you send a newsletter, promote your Facebook feed. Ensure that your loyal readers know about it and can easily subscribe! Always provide a link so they can click and follow.

**MENTION IT ON YOUR CONTACT PAGE**
On your "contact us" page mention your Facebook feed. That way people who are interested in you can easily follow you. The same thing for any "about us" page. Always have a clickable link.

## THE VALUE OF FOLLOWERS

When you look at a Facebook account, it's easy to get caught up in the follower or friend count. However, how many followers you have is only one aspect of the power of your Facebook account. Here's why.

Yes, the number of followers you have indicates the number of people who directly see your Facebook posts when they check their main Facebook feed. They see posts made by the people they follow. If they follow 10 people, this could be great. If they follow 10,000 people, this could mean you are completely lost in the flood of messages they receive.

However, Facebook is far beyond a simple concept of followers. Facebook is a massive database of content. Here is how it really works.

How most people use Facebook like this. They hang out in their timeline. They see what their friends are posting. They also see what their friends are commenting on. So let's say Jim Bob Smith likes your post about green peas. He writes a funny comment on your post. Now all 5,000 of Jim Bob's friends see the comment. A bunch of them click to see what this is all about. Now they've learned about your page. Now they may chime in and join you.

And some people do search the Facebook system looking for things. So even if you aren't connected by friends or fans, you can still be found.

So yes, followers are nice. They are people who might see the post you've made. But even if you don't have a lot of followers, your posts can have a huge reach. All you have to do is make popular-topic or fun posts that those millions of readers are looking for, and you will be automatically picked up by them, read, and your news will be paid attention to.

## COLLABORATE WITH FRIENDS

If you've got friends on Facebook in your same topic area, work with them to help each other out. Mention each other in your posts. Like each other's posts. Mention each other's feeds in your newsletters and other social media posts.

If your own newsletter has 1,000 members on it and you have 5 friends who each have 1,000 members, suddenly you've quadrupled your reach – and so have they.

## FOLLOWERS WHO BOTHER YOU

There's always going to be that follower that harasses you for some reason. Sends you spam or annoying messages. Maybe they're an erotic model who posts nude photos of themselves.

For whatever reason, you always have the option to block someone.

Blocking someone makes them unable to post to you, message you, or show up on any of your pages.

Simply go to their profile, click on the three-dots ("more") icon on the right, and you can block them.

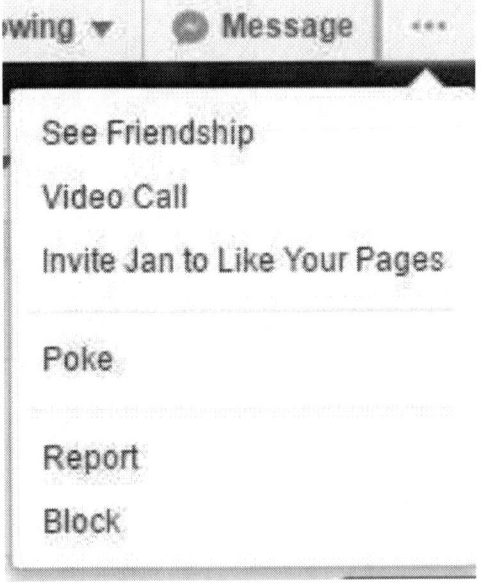

## POTENTIAL CONTACTS WHO WON'T ACCEPT

It's going to happen. There's that contact that you really want to connect with. But they just won't accept your request.

Why?

First off, make sure they follow *anybody* back. Some Facebook accounts, for a variety of personal reasons, refuse to connect. If the account you're chasing has only five connections, stop holding your breath. It's just not how they operate. Accept that they might read and like but they just won't follow. Find other things to focus your energies on.

What if they have a fairly good number of connections – maybe 2000 – but they just won't connect with *you*? It might be that your own follow notice got lost in the pile. It happens. People sometimes forget to check that area of the site.

First, make sure you like and comment on their posts. Each time you do that they get a notification. If they're a reasonably attentive Facebook user they'll eventually click to see what you're about. They'll realize they aren't following you and they'll follow you back.

Let's say you like and comment actively for a few weeks but they're still not responding. The next step is to take a look at their posts. Do they look robotic? Do they look like they're auto-posting from Twitter? It might be that the user doesn't even realize what is happening on their Facebook account because some robotic script is handling everything for them. In that case, figure out where they're really posting from. If all their posts have a Twitter URL in them, go like them on Twitter. Talk with them there. And, once you get a conversation going, mention that you'd like to connect on Facebook as well. That might give them the nudge they need to log on. Which they should be doing anyway.

I would definitely not recommend posting harassing messages in your comments saying "Follow me!!" or sending them direct messages. The moment you cross into the "I want to pressure you into following me" category they're likely to resist. You want to lure them into doing it. The carrot works far better than the stick.

## CHAPTER 13 – MESSAGES

Private messages in Facebook are fairly straightforward. In fact, there's a big MESSAGE button beneath each user's profile. Here's how to use it.

## MESSAGES BASICS

Go to a user's profile. Right on their profile page is a big MESSAGE button.

You'll get a pop-up box to type a message into.

Type your message and hit return. Off it goes.

Hit "send" and you're set. The messages all show up in the "Messages" section, which is an icon in the top of your menu bar.

## WHO YOU CAN MESSAGE?

You can message someone that isn't blocking you by typing in their name.

The recipient will see their "messaging" notification icon light up to indicate they have gotten a message.

You can talk back and forth just like in any texting / messaging type of application.

Note that you have the option of blocking and reporting users in here, just in case somebody does bother you.

## CHAPTER 14 – GROUPS

Groups are collections of people interested in a topic. There are groups for yoga. Groups for meditation. Groups for Crime Fiction authors. Groups for promoting and marketing books. You name it and there's probably a group.

If you're an author, I have an Excel spreadsheet of good book marketing groups to join:

http://www.lisashea.com/lisabase/writing/gettingyourbookpublished/facebookgroups.html

Why have a group rather than a business page?

A business page only allows the owner of that page to make an initial post. Others can comment on it, but they can't make their own posts. With a group, anybody who is a member can post. It means there are more conversations.

Joining a group or two is a great way to meet like-minded people who might be interested in the products you have. Just do a few searches to track down groups related to your interests.

You can also make your own groups.

Here's how to get started.

## CREATING A GROUP

Go to any existing group page. For example, I run a book discussion group called BookKitten:

https://www.facebook.com/groups/bookkitten/

It looks like this:

On the lower right of that page is a button to create a group. Groups have fewer options than pages because they can't post elsewhere or like or share things "as the group". Everyone who posts in a group does so as their actual personal page. You can't belong to a group as a business page nor post there as a business page. So groups are solely about actual personal accounts making posts and talking.

On the up side, everyone in the group can start conversations. So it's a good way for a group of authors to share news about their books, for example.

You lose a lot of functionality with groups, though. You can't like pages as a group. You can't make posts on pages as a group. You have to trust the members not to post highly inappropriate things.

So give thought to whether you really want to have a group rather than a business page.

## CHAPTER 15 - ADVANCED TIPS

Practice with Facebook every day. Get a sense of how liking, commenting, and posting all work.

When you've got a handle on those basics, it's time to move on to a few advanced topics!

## OPTIMAL IMAGES FOR LIKES

Let me first caveat to say that your image feed should be about your brand, whatever it is. If you are an oil painter who does landscapes, post photos of those paintings. If you're an author of Alabama mysteries, post photos of your covers and of beautiful Alabama landscapes as you walk around doing your research. That is what your followers will expect.

Having said that, there are also some interesting trends in what users on Facebook tend to click on and to like. They are, users are drawn to things that are:

- Light in color rather than dark
- Blue

The light in color probably has to do with how the smartphone and tablet work. Something dark on there is just harder to see. There's a reason we don't read white text against a black background. So a lighter image is easier on the eye and more likely to be examined.

Why blue? Isn't red the color that draws the eye? Who knows. Maybe it's the deep blue sea or the clear blue sky. Whatever the reason, viewers tend to be slightly more drawn to images with blue.

So if your paintings are all jagged red shapes against a black background, I would never recommend altering them just for a few more Facebook likes. However, if you intersperse motivational quotes with your paintings, I'd recommend making those on a light blue background. It'll draw in readers who will then stay to look at your other items.

## MOTIVATIONAL QUOTES

As mentioned earlier, motivational quotes are quite popular not only on Facebook but on all social networking feeds. It lifts a person up. It makes them feel good. It gives them an extra push on whatever they're doing.

Unless your business focus is to do motivational quotes, I wouldn't post ONLY the quotes. And I would focus on quotes in your topic area. If you're an author, putting up quotes occasionally about writing and overcoming writer's block would be perfect. Maybe some for readers as well.

Think about your topic area and what kind of quotes your visitors would enjoy. Are you a cat toy company? Use fun quotes about cats.

Just keep those backgrounds light blue ;).

## USE THE WORD "LIKE"

This gets into the bizarre realm of psychology. People are fairly easily "cued" by words to think things. If you keep talking about yawns and yawning, a portion of readers are likely to feel an urge to yawn. The same is true, oddly enough, with the word "like."

You don't have to say "I need you to like my post!!!" – that would be considered a bit pushy. Instead, work the word "like" into your general description.

So you could for example say:

"My new murder mystery story is like Agatha Christie having a love child with Robert B. Parker!"

Just the word "like" existing in their sentence primes them to push the like button.

Marketers around the world know and use these subtle techniques, so it's worth a try occasionally. Just don't lean on it too heavily! Quality content will always win over convoluted psych games ☺.

## GETTING MORE COMMENTS

Comments are a key to building interest in your images. How do you get comments? You need to ask for them.

Some artists get grumpy about comments and users can get shy about speaking up if they don't know the artist in question. So make it clear on each post that you're interested in feedback.

In addition to asking explicitly for that feedback, pose a question as well.

It can be an actual one, like shown here, or it can be a more open-ended one about whether they like the image or if they think you should have zoomed in closer or something like that. Ask anything at all. It'll get people responding.

## PLAY WITH DIFFERENT TIMES

You'll see some people swear that 2am is the absolute ideal time to make posts to get lots of attention. Others swear it's 5pm. However, what if your perfect target market is soccer moms in New York City who tend to go to bed at 9pm? Maybe their one time to surf the phone is over coffee at 7am.

Only *you* will know when your target audience is active – and your way to find that out is by testing.

Rowdy 20-somethings out clubbing in Miami have a different schedule than elderly cat-owners in London. Your group might be an early or late group. They might have a few peak times.

Make posts at different times of day and keep track of how many responses you get at each time. You'll see patterns fairly quickly and they'll be unique to the people you are going after. Yes, you can watch other people in your topic area and see what they do, and see how the responses go. But in the end it comes down to you and your own fan base. Listen to them. Pay attention to their habits.

## RUN CONTESTS

People love to win things. It's human nature. Running contests is a popular way to bring in fans. Just make sure you do it legally.

Many countries have laws against contests. And while you might think "Who will sue me for a contest" you might be surprised. If you gather personal information from a minor that can easily violate many laws.

The safest thing to do is do some quick research on the basics of running a web contest. Usually it involves stating it's for adults 18 or older in the US and UK only. If you live somewhere else, research the laws in your country. There needs to be a set start time, end time, and prize. The prize value must be declared.

You must draw the entry randomly. Find a random number generator online and use it.

## CHAPTER 16 – ISSUES TO AVOID

We've talked quite a lot about the ways to best use Facebook. Now here's some advice about issues to watch out for.

## STEALING CONTENT

It is fine to accompany a post with a stock image that you own the rights to. That is accepted and normal on Facebook. However, don't post an entire article that you copied from someone else. That is theft. You can LINK to their article on their website. But you can't just cut-and-paste their content and then post it into Facebook as if you wrote it.

Also, while stock images to go with a link or blurb are considered fine, avoid posting images that give them impression that YOU took them. That is also not kosher.

## REPEATED HAMMERING OF A TAG

It's fine to post daily. It's even fine to post a few things in a row if you're working on a project. But posting all day long in a key word tag is generally found to be annoying. People are on Facebook because they want to enjoy a wealth of voices, not one person "hogging the feed."

Be a good community member. Start slow and build up as you get used to the system.

## BANNING

Facebook can enact either temporary or permanent bans on accounts that they feel are misbehaving. Misbehaving includes hateful language, behavior that seems to be harassment, and similar issues.

Be aware that your posts are able to be reported by other users. If enough other users are upset with your posts, and Facebook agrees with them, your account could suffer. It's worth it to follow Facebook guidelines.

## CHAPTER 17 - MULTIPLE ACCOUNTS

Most other systems like Twitter, Instagram, Pinterest, and so on highly encourage you to have multiple accounts.

Not Facebook.

Facebook expects you to have one and only one account for yourself as a person. This account is about you as a person.

You are not supposed to have fake accounts or pen name accounts.

You can create "business pages" which we talked about previously – and also "group pages" - that is where you can do discussions for a group or activity. But those are NOT a personal profile.

## CHAPTER 18 – ACTUALLY READING POSTS

If you do choose to friend people and follow pages with your personal account, once you start following a few hundred people, you'll see the high rate at which posts can stream past your eyeballs. You can barely keep up with the flow.

How do people actually read the posts coming in at them?

## SEARCH KEY WORDS

Searching is the key way to get just a subgroup of posts. You can search on cyanotypes or watercolors, on cozymystery or sweetromance. Whatever your interest is, do the search and see what you find.

## CHAPTER 19 –FACEBOOK ADS

I avoid paying for ads as much as possible. In all of my social networking books, I have never advocated paying for ads.

Facebook ads are the one exception.

You can get HUGE amounts of traffic for your products if you properly use Facebook ads.

I could write an entire book on all the details and techniques involved in precisely honing a Facebook ad, but let's cover the basics here.

## CREATING A FACEBOOK AD

Let me say first that creating a Facebook ad is NOT BOOSTING A POST. Avoid the boost option, as much as Facebook continually rams it at you. Instead, go to the Down-Arrow icon in the top right of your page and from the drop down choose "Create Ads".

Facebook is continually changing their ad interface in order to confuse as many clients as possible ☺. Just hang in there. It currently looks like this:

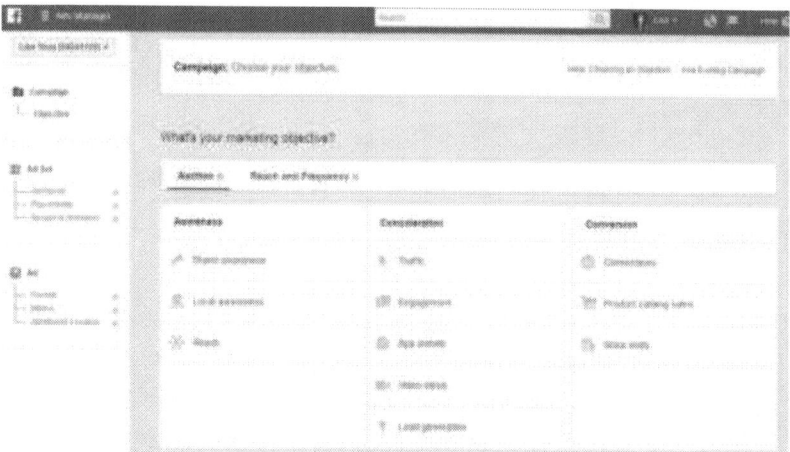

Stay with auction and choose Brand Awareness. You want to target as precisely as possible the people you show your ad to in order to get the best results. No need to pay to show your ad to someone who is not at all interested in your type of product.

Give this campaign a name – this is just for your own tracking.

The system will next ask you about a lookalike audience. Let's say you have a page with 3,000 loyal fans who love your product. Facebook will examine those 3,000 fans and figure out what they have in common. This can be a great way to then reach other similar people in Facebook who will probably love your product, too.

But unless you have a decent number of fans already, this is something to hold off on.

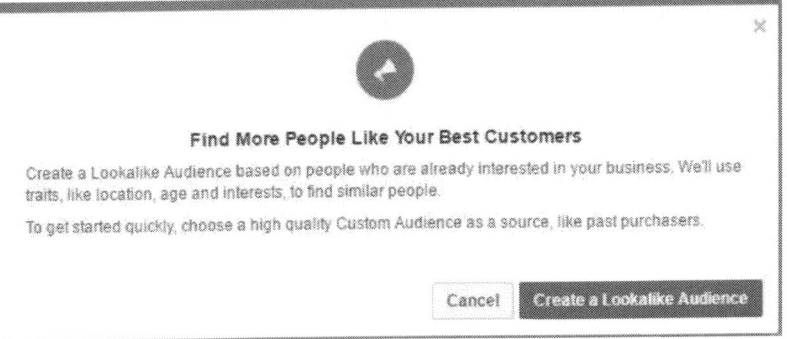

Just to show you what it would do, though, it would then ask for which page to match the lookalike against. I'd choose my Lisa Shea Author page. I can then geo-target people to just one location and choose the percentage of that population I'd like to work with.

So in this case I am going to take just 1% of the US population – the 1% most precisely like my existing fans. I would then use that as the start of any marketing efforts.

Now it's time to start defining the market for your ad more precisely.

## DEFINING YOUR AD MARKET

The top half of your audience page talks about the general demographics to show your ad to. In my case I'm making an ad for a romance novel. You might think it's only young people, but actually my novels do quite well with older people. So I am leaving the age range wide open, but only showing it to women. I'm also focusing in on the US only since I'll be using a US-Amazon link. I could then make separate ads for the UK and so on if I wished.

So here is the starting point.

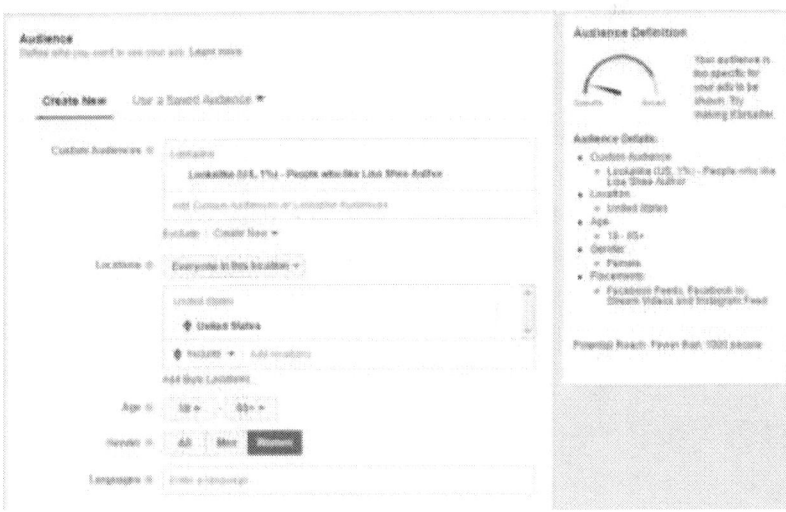

But now we get into the important part. Or the *more* important part.

We have to choose specific interests these people have. My romance novel in question is a sweetly clean, no sex, medieval romance. So people who hate clean romances would hate mine. I need to make sure I target my book precisely to those readers who appreciate clean romances.

I've scrolled the page down a little to show the next section.

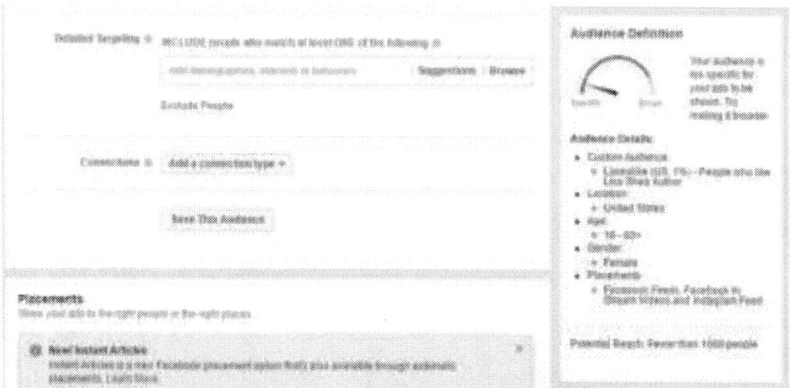

It's that "detailed targeting" spot which is critical. You must put in items related to your own product. And they must be as perfectly targeted as possible.

Let's say I put "Game of Thrones" in there.

You might think, wonderful! There are 38 \*\*million\*\* people who have that interest! I've hit the mother lode!

But there are two big problems here.

First, Game of Thrones is a TV show. There are LOTS and LOTS of people who watch TV and hate reading. You always want to target your specific area. If you're a book writer, that means books. If you're an artist, that means other artists.

Second, while Game of Thrones is sort of medieval in theme, it's fantasy and it's full of sex. Someone who adores the fantasy sex aspect might hate my book for being realistic and clean (no sex).

So let's try something else. How about Outlander, which is far more realistic and, while not set in medieval times, is close in a historical sense.

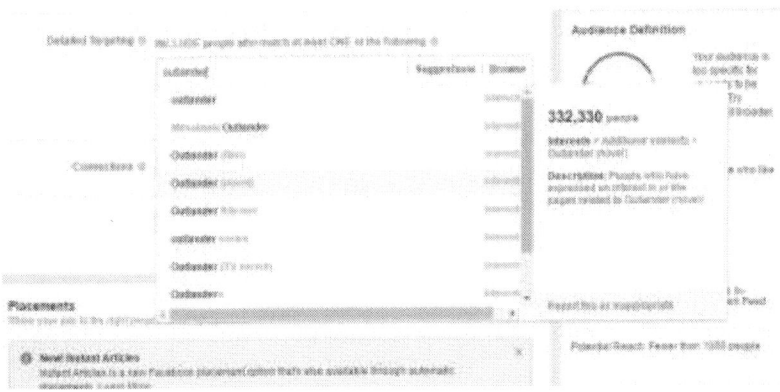

OK, we have fewer matches but they're better targeted. Also note that you have choices there for Outlander the novel,

Outlander the TV series, and so on. You always want to find the novel link if at all possible (if you're an author). You can waste a lot of money if you target a group which just isn't interested in what you're offering.

A lot of people who complain about not getting a lot of clicks have issues right here. They are targeting people who have no interest in their product because the terms they used were too vague.

Outlander, of course, does have fairly extreme sex and violence, so it's still not a great match for me.

OK, how about Tanya Ann Crosby who writes medieval novels? They might be sexy but at least we're getting closer –

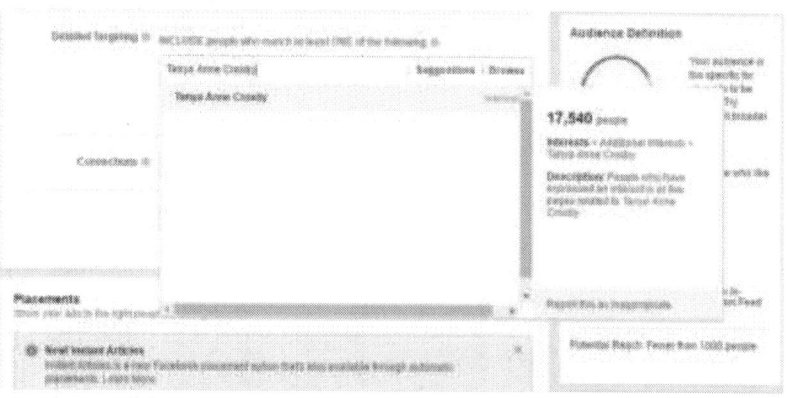

That's starting to do it.

You will add in a number of different authors (or companies or whatever) to make this work. Just keep searching them out and adding them in. This is where it's critical to know your product well and to know what other items are similar. No product in the world is unique, as much as we authors / artists / entrepreneurs like to think they are. There are always other authors who have a similar writing style. Other worlds which have similarities. You need to find those, understand them, and use them.

Next up, we look into where this ad will be shown.

# AD PLACEMENTS

Your ad can run on both Facebook and Instagram –

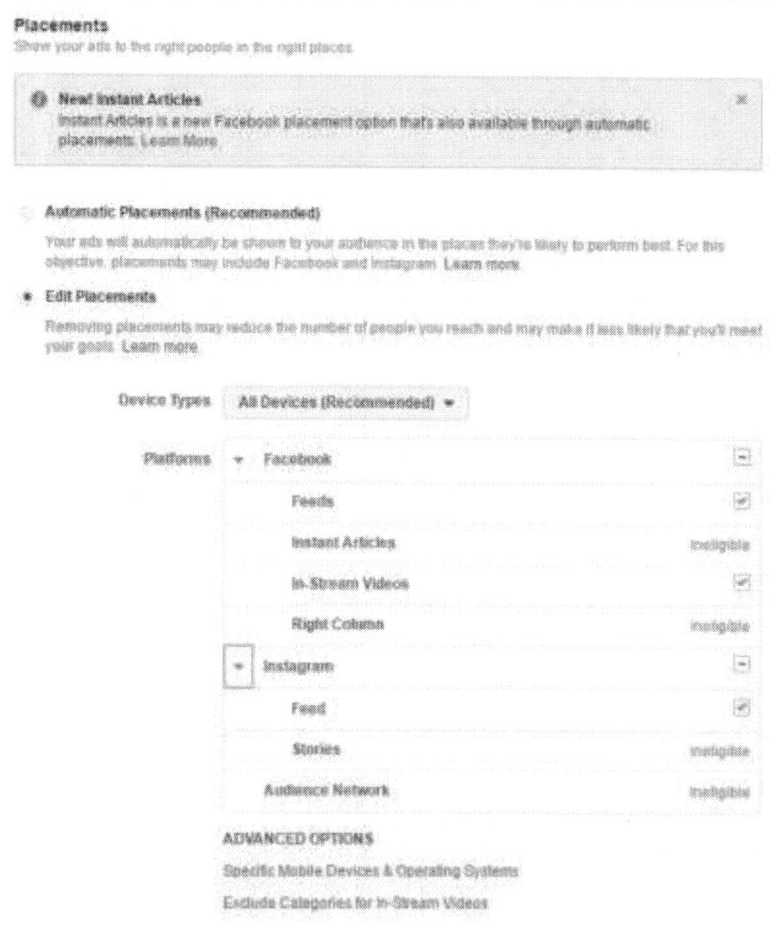

In my case, I'm advertising a book and that book can be bought by anybody from any device. I definitely want to reach both Facebook and Instagram. I recommend using the large reach unless you have a compelling reason to avoid Instagram. I'm not sure what that would be. Maybe if you were specifically wanting to advertise a Facebook page in order to get it to have more fans. But for any other product-type of promotion, go for the wide range.

## AD BUDGET

This is of course a sensitive topic for many people. Certainly start small. But also realize that part of what you're doing here is a testing process. You'll see if one author name (or whatever you're using) works well. Then try another one. You'll try one graphic. Another graphic. One tag line. As you optimize, you will save a ton of money because your ads will turn into clicks in a flurry – and you'll get a lot of sales. You'll be making money, not spending money.

But you have to start somewhere.

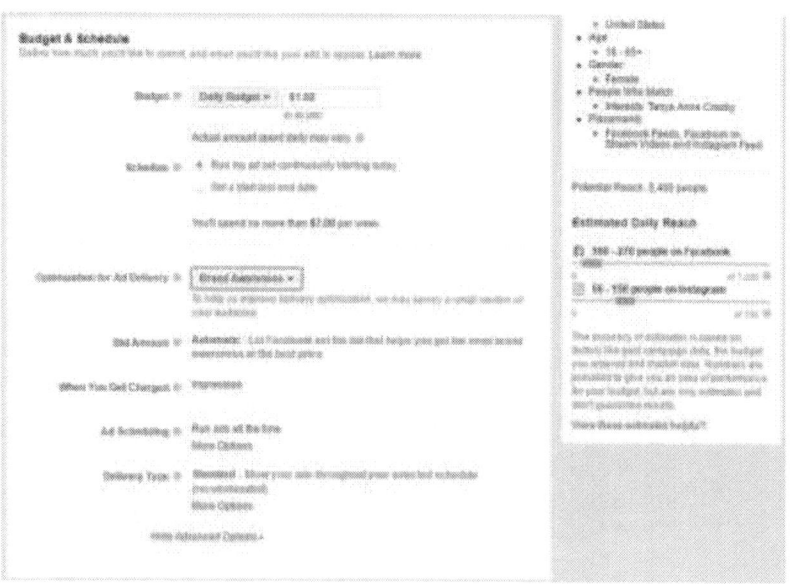

Let the system auto-bid based on the key word you chose. Note that popular key words will have more competition than lesser-used key words, so that's another reason to be attentive in your research. If the entire world is bidding for Game of Thrones you'll pay a lot to be in that mix. If nobody at all is bidding for the novelist you chose, you'll be paying pennies.

At the very bottom, give this ad set (combination of parameters) a name and hit CONTINUE.

## AD DESIGN

The design of your ad is absolutely critical. Test after test after test show that even subtle changes in an ad can create huge differences in click rates.

Your ad CANNOT LOOK LIKE AN AD at first glance. Otherwise people will scroll on past it. Instead, it has to look like an appealing image. Don't show your book cover! Show an image from the book. Don't show a box! Show the beautiful soap sitting in a lovely soap dish.

Here's a well-performing ad for one of my books.

Let's go through the details.

First – always choose to have just one image. One. Period. You need your one, best, most perfect image to show to them. If you try carousels or other things you are going to lose them. People scroll and click. Show them the absolute most perfect image that will catch their eye.

Avoid text or promos or anything else on that image. I went through test after test to come down to this one. Often it's the balance of light and dark. The direction the eye moves in.

You want to lead the eye down and right to the DOWNLOAD button (or whatever button you choose). That is the most important part. See how your eyes start on his face, go down into her face, and then sort of follow down to her shoulder? That's what you want. Create an image that has that top-left to bottom-right flow.

Next up – the top blurb. These needs to be short, powerful, and meaningful. Don't go for esoteric here. Avoid bland! And always ask them to share. Their sharing gets you thousands and thousands of FREE views as all their friends take a look. Sharing is critical. You need to ask for it.

Next, the below-banner headline. Again, keep this short, snappy, and powerful. Catch their eye and attention.

Finally, the text blurb. You have two lines at the most. This needs again to be punchy, interesting, and alluring. Don't "tell" them the storyline like you're writing a book report. Create an atmosphere. Lure them in.

For books, you want the link to go directly to a sale page and for the button to say download. If you send them anywhere else, like to your Facebook page or webpage or so on, you're going to lose buyers along the way. Go right for the jugular. Send them immediately to where they can click buy.

## THE REVIEW PROCESS

The ad is going to be reviewed by a human being to make sure it's appropriate for Facebook. They don't like pornography showing to people, for example.

Sometime within 24 hours you should get a note that your ad is going live.

That's when it's time to go to the Ads Manager to watch how your ads are doing.

## ADS MANAGER

In the top-right "down arrow" menu, click on "Manage Ads" to get to your ads you're running. Click on your name to enter your account.

You'll be shown a page that shows how much you spent a day, what campaigns are running, how many clicks you've gotten, and about how much you're spending per click.

Here's some tests I'm running. So on this screen you get an overview of what's going on.

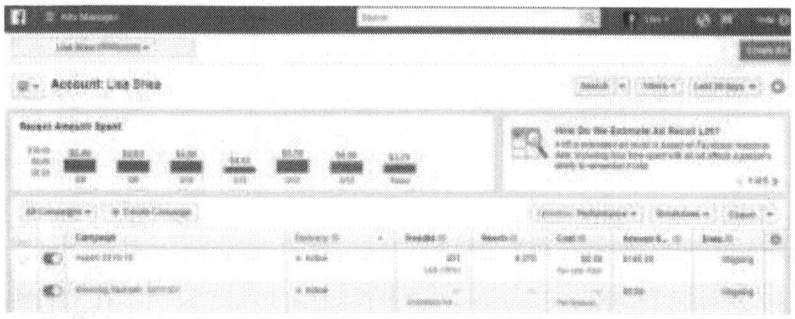

Click on any Campaign name to then see the details for that campaign. So let's click on Aspen, for my Aspen Allegations mystery story.

# Facebook for Authors, Artists, and Entrepreneurs

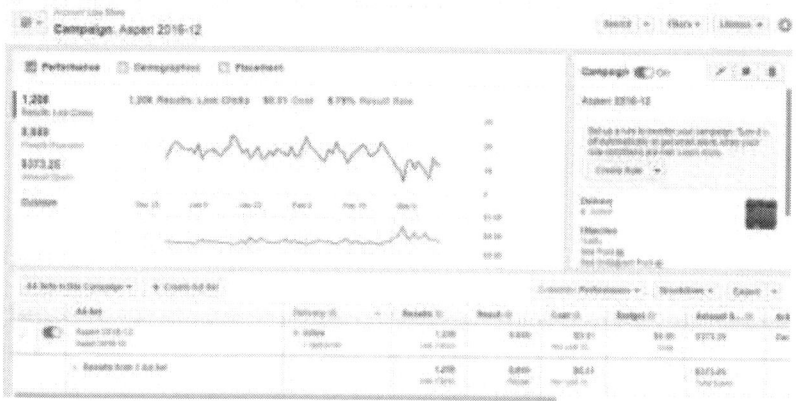

This is one I set up as a test and unfortunately forgot about. So it's been getting a relatively high rate of 31 cents per click and is recently spiking higher. Maybe other people came across the novels I was using for my targeted interests and started bidding against me? There are all sorts of reasons the climate can change in advertising. You need to look at your stats every few days and be ready to make adjustments. I clearly should have started adjusting things on March 1st when the numbers began changing.

Ads are never a set-and-forget solution. The ad world changes regularly. Popular key words change. The people who are bidding against you change. Keep notes and find the combination that works perfectly for your product. But don't assume it's eternal. Be ready to tweak.

## CHANGING AN AD

This part is critical to understand.

Let's say I have my Aspen Allegations ad which looks like this:

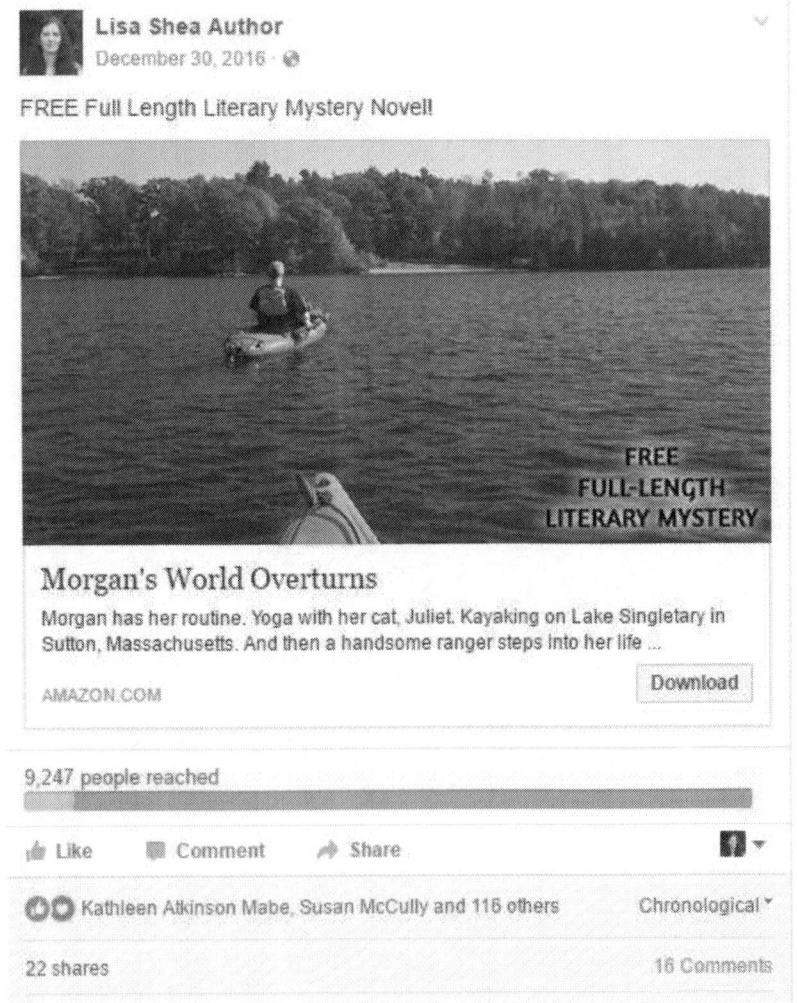

It's got tons of likes. It's got lots of share, and a handful of comments.

If I edit that ad's look or feel in ANY WAY – all of that goes away.

Why?

Imagine I had 118 people all visibly saying they liked the ad. And now I change the image so it's nearly pornographic. All those people are now publicly attached to a nearly pornographic image without even knowing it.

Imagine I changed the ad text to promote something hateful.

You can see how this could be abused.

So you never want to change the look or feel of an ad. You'll lose all its existing value. When you do a new test, make a new ad.

The thing you CAN change is the demographics. You can change the age range, the targeted interests, and that sort of stuff without losing the existing likes and comments. The ad itself is remaining the same.

Still, though, I wouldn't do that either. When you're running tests, you need to do them completely cleanly. You need a fresh ad running with the fresh settings to see how it does.

That's because the existence of those likes and shares make a difference. That is, if someone sees an ad scroll by that has 500 likes on it, they get a good feeling. They know the ad is one people like. They're more likely to like it themselves.

But if an ad scrolls by with ZERO likes, it makes the person a bit suspicious. It's like going by a restaurant with no patrons. It makes you wonder if something's wrong with the restaurant.

So those likes and shares make an impression. They influence how people react to the ad. To properly compare ad setups you need to have each one start from scratch in the exact same way, to see how they perform against each other.

A lot of marketers skip over this testing step. They simply throw up an ad and then complain when it is charging them enormous money for no results.

In the meantime, other people are making tens of thousands of dollars a month by using Facebook ads to drive killer traffic to their products. They get their per-click rate down to pennies and get stellar results per click.

It's all about investing that time. Finding the absolute perfect ad for the absolute perfect audience.

Good luck!

## CHAPTER 20 - LISA'S ACCOUNT

To get a sense of how I post, here is a link to my main account.

https://www.facebook.com/lisashea.origami

Here is my BookKitten group, to see how a group works:

https://www.facebook.com/groups/bookkitten/

Here are a number of my business pages, so you can see how those work.

https://www.facebook.com/LisaSheaAuthor

https://www.facebook.com/bostonwriters/

https://www.facebook.com/RomanceClassLove/

https://www.facebook.com/BVArtAssoc/

https://www.facebook.com/farfromeden

https://www.facebook.com/BellaOnline-323931250391/

https://www.facebook.com/bellaonlinelowcarb

## CHAPTER 21 - SUMMARY

Facebook is similar to many other social networks out there – but its focus has been on building connections for business purposes. This means it's perfect for authors, artists, and entrepreneurs looking to get more fans for the things they are producing.

It only takes a few minutes a day and the results can be quite useful to your dreams!

Best of luck!

Thank you for reading this *Facebook for Authors, Artists and Entrepreneurs* book! I hope you found some new tools which can help you in your marketing efforts.

If you found some of this information to be useful, please leave a review – I'd appreciate it immensely!

You can also post reviews on Goodreads and any other systems you use. Together we can help make a difference!

If you have a tip I didn't cover, please let me know! Together we can help each other build our skills.

FREE books in my library include:

## FREE EBOOKS

If one of these is not free on your system for some strange book-vendor-being-cranky reason, all author's proceeds will go to support battered women's shelters.

Be sure to sign up for my free newsletter! You'll get alerts of free books, discounts, and new releases. I run my own newsletter server – nobody else will ever see your email address. I promise!

http://www.lisashea.com/lisabase/subscribe.html

## DEDICATION

Thank you so much to the members of the Blackstone Valley Art Association who helped me with details.

To the Boston Writer's Group, who supports me in all my projects. Tom H offered good feedback.

My Sutton Writing Group is also quite helpful.

Megan M offered some great suggestions.

To my boyfriend, who encourages me in all of my dreams.

Most of all, to my loyal fans on GoodReads, Facebook, Twitter, Google+, and other systems who encourage me. Thank you so much for your enthusiasm!

## GLOSSARY

Block – the ability to prevent a person from following you or contacting you. You will never see their posts in your timeline.

Message – a personal message sent from one account to another.

Friend– the basic form of connection on Facebook. When you connect with someone, their posts are visible in your general timeline view and vice versa.

Follower – A relatively new concept for Facebook - someone who has chosen to get news of any posts you post.

Like – showing your appreciation for a post. The post then shows up in your list of "likes."

Facebook– a social networking / college student platform first launched in February 2004.

Share – distributing information about a post to your own network of followers.

## ABOUT THE AUTHOR

Lisa has always enjoyed helping others achieve their dreams in writing. She has owned BellaOnline for over fifteen years now. BellaOnline is a free training system for writers which teaches them everything from time management to clear writing to social networking. She publishes a quarterly literary magazine. She runs two separate writing groups to help both fiction and non-fiction authors achieve their goals.

One of Lisa's mantras is that we all help each other succeed. Authors are not in competition with each other. We are all here to elevate the selection of books available to our audience. Every voice deserves to be heard. Every author has a story to tell.

Together we all thrive!

A portion of my proceeds from my books benefit battered women's shelters.

Please visit the following pages for news about free books, discounted releases, and new launches. Feel free to post questions there – I strive to answer within a day!

Facebook:
https://www.facebook.com/LisaSheaAuthor

Twitter:
https://twitter.com/LisaSheaAuthor

Google+:
https://plus.google.com/+LisaSheaAuthor/posts

GoodReads:
https://www.goodreads.com/lisashea/

Blog:
http://www.lisashea.com/lisabase/blog/

Newsletter:
http://www.lisashea.com/lisabase/subscribe.html

Share the news – we all want to enjoy interesting books!

Made in the USA
Lexington, KY
08 June 2017